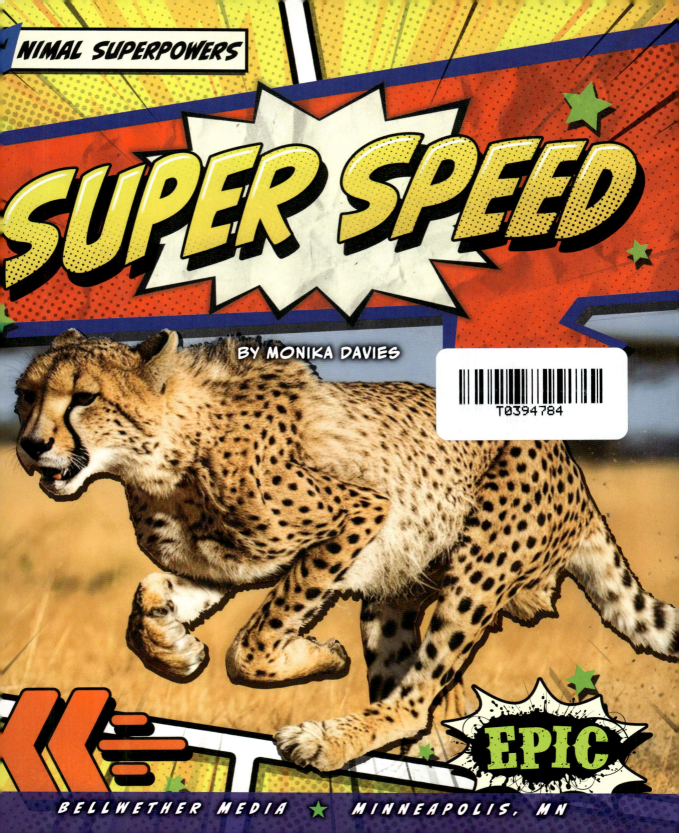

**EPIC BOOKS** are no ordinary books. They burst with intense action, high-speed heroics, and shadows of the unknown. Are you ready for an Epic adventure?

This edition first published in 2026 by Bellwether Media, Inc.

No part of this publication may be reproduced in whole or in part without written permission of the publisher. For information regarding permission, write to Bellwether Media, Inc., Attention: Permissions Department, 3500 American Blvd W, Suite 150, Bloomington, MN 55431.

Library of Congress Cataloging-in-Publication Data

LC record for Super Speed available at: https://lccn.loc.gov/2025021815

Text copyright © 2026 by Bellwether Media, Inc. EPIC and associated logos are trademarks and/or registered trademarks of Bellwether Media, Inc. Bellwether Media is a division of FlutterBee Education Group.

Editor: Rachael Barnes    Designer: Gabriel Hilger

Printed in the United States of America, North Mankato, MN.

# TABLE OF CONTENTS

THE SPEEDSTERS ................... 4
CHEETAH CHASE ..................... 6
SPEEDY SAILFISH ................. 10
FLYING MAMMAL ...................14
ONE FAST FALCON ............... 18
GLOSSARY ............................. 22
TO LEARN MORE ................... 23
INDEX ..................................... 24

# THE SPEEDSTERS

Many animals are speedsters. They move fast! Some can **sprint**. Others can swim or fly for miles. Some dash to catch **prey**. Others are quick to escape danger. Their speed is a super skill.

# CHEETAH CHASE

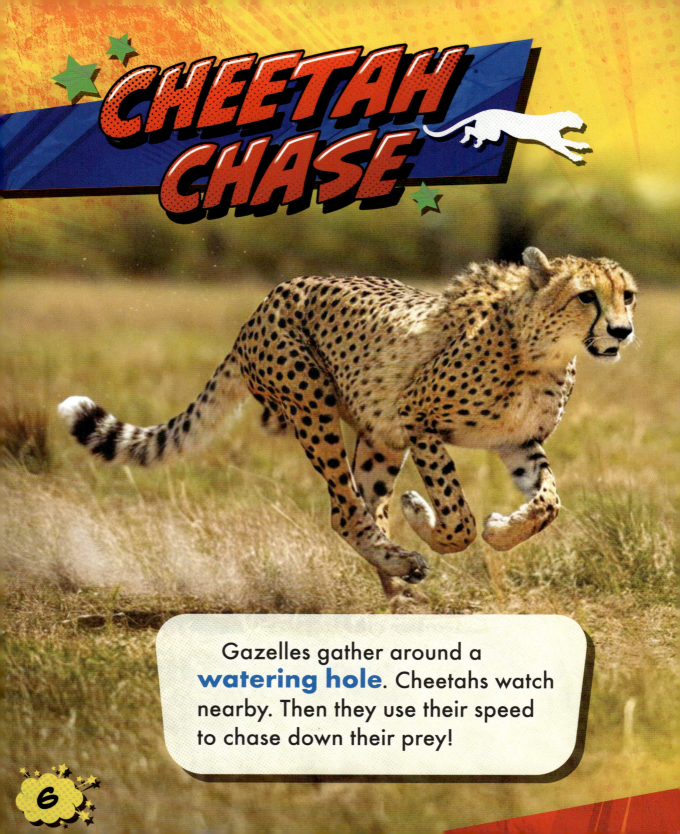

Gazelles gather around a **watering hole**. Cheetahs watch nearby. Then they use their speed to chase down their prey!

Cheetahs have **flexible** spines. They can take long **strides**. Their tails help them balance and turn quickly.

## CHEETAH

CLASS: MAMMAL

LIFE SPAN: 8 TO 12 YEARS

### STATUS IN THE WILD

| LEAST CONCERN | NEAR THREATENED | VULNERABLE | ENDANGERED | CRITICALLY ENDANGERED | EXTINCT IN THE WILD | EXTINCT |

### RANGE

## SLOW TO SPEEDY
Cheetahs can go from standing to running 60 miles (97 kilometers) per hour in three seconds!

**CLAWS**

Cheetahs' short claws **grip** the ground while running. Their long legs help them easily sprint.

**SPRINT IN ACTION!**

**LONG TAIL** — HELPS THEM STAY BALANCED WHEN RUNNING FAST

**FLEXIBLE SPINE** — HELPS THEM TAKE LONGER STEPS AND LEAPS

**CLAWS** — HELP THEM GRIP THE GROUND

Cheetahs are the fastest land **mammals**. They can run up to 75 miles (121 kilometers) per hour!

# SPEEDY SAILFISH

DORSAL FIN

Sailfish are known for their large **dorsal fins**. These fins are often taller than the length of their bodies!

Sailfish circle **schools** of fish. Their fins can push their prey closer together.

# SAILFISH

**CLASS: FISH**

**LIFE SPAN:**

**UP TO 15 YEARS**

## STATUS IN THE WILD

| LEAST CONCERN | NEAR THREATENED | VULNERABLE | ENDANGERED | CRITICALLY ENDANGERED | EXTINCT IN THE WILD | EXTINCT |

### RANGE

When sailfish are ready to attack, they fold down their dorsal fins. This helps them move faster.

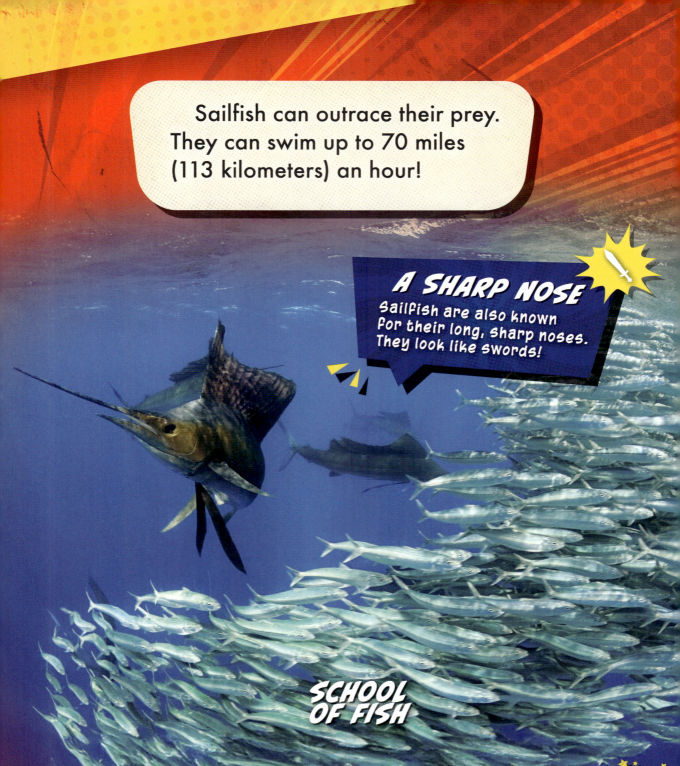

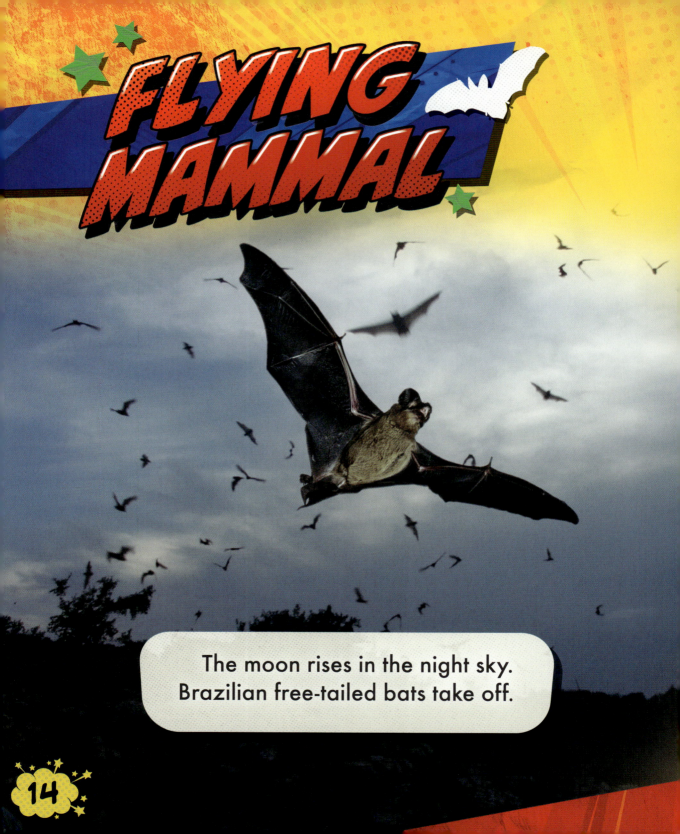

The bats fly in a tight group. They travel over 30 miles (48 kilometers) tonight to feed!

# BRAZILIAN FREE-TAILED BAT

**CLASS: MAMMAL**

**LIFE SPAN: AROUND 8 YEARS**

## STATUS IN THE WILD

| LEAST CONCERN | NEAR THREATENED | VULNERABLE | ENDANGERED | CRITICALLY ENDANGERED | EXTINCT IN THE WILD | EXTINCT |

**RANGE**

Brazilian free-tailed bats fly fast. They can **glide** over 99 miles (159 kilometers) per hour!

ONE-OF-A-KIND
Bats are the only mammals that can fly!

MOTH

Their long, narrow wings help them fly quickly. Their fast flight allows them to catch moths.

# ONE FAST FALCON

A peregrine falcon circles in the sky. It spots a pigeon.

The falcon pulls in its wings and tail. It dives! When it gets close, the falcon's claws hit and catch its next meal.

# PEREGRINE FALCON

**CLASS: BIRD**

**LIFE SPAN: UP TO 20 YEARS**

## STATUS IN THE WILD

| LEAST CONCERN | NEAR THREATENED | VULNERABLE | ENDANGERED | CRITICALLY ENDANGERED | EXTINCT IN THE WILD | EXTINCT |

**RANGE**

Peregrine falcons are the fastest animal on Earth. They can dive at over 200 miles (322 kilometers) per hour! This dive is called a stoop.

**TEARDROP SHAPE**
PULLING IN THEIR WINGS, TALONS, AND TAIL TO DIVE FASTER

**STIFF FEATHERS**
CUT THROUGH THE AIR EASILY

**STOOP IN ACTION!**

Speedy animals can be found all around!

## FAST FEATHERS
These falcons have stiff feathers on their wings. Their feathers easily cut through the air.

# GLOSSARY

**dorsal fins**—fins on top of a sailfish's back; sailfish have two dorsal fins.

**flexible**—able to bend

**glide**—to move smoothly

**grip**—to hold tightly

**mammals**—warm-blooded animals that have backbones and feed their young milk

**prey**—animals that are hunted by other animals for food

**schools**—groups of fish

**sprint**—to run at full speed

**strides**—very long steps

**watering hole**—a pool of water from which animals drink

# TO LEARN MORE

### AT THE LIBRARY

Chang, Kirsten. *Cheetah or Leopard?* Minneapolis, Minn.: Bellwether Media, 2020.

Greve, Meg. *Super-fast Animals.* Mankato, Minn.: Black Rabbit Books, 2025.

Marie, Renata. *Amazing Animal Speed.* Minneapolis, Minn.: Kaleidoscope, 2021.

### ON THE WEB

# FACTSURFER

Factsurfer.com gives you a safe, fun way to find more information.

1. Go to www.factsurfer.com.

2. Enter "super speed" into the search box and click 🔍.

3. Select your book cover to see a list of related content.

# INDEX

attack, 12
bodies, 10
Brazilian free-tailed bats, 14, 15, 16, 17
cheetahs, 6, 7, 8, 9
claws, 8, 19
dive, 19, 20
dorsal fins, 10, 11, 12
escape, 4
feathers, 21
fly, 4, 15, 16, 17
legs, 8
mammals, 9, 16
noses, 13
peregrine falcons, 18, 19, 20, 21
prey, 4, 6, 11, 13, 17, 18
range, 7, 11, 15, 19
run, 8, 9
sailfish, 10, 11, 12, 13
speed, 4, 6, 8, 9, 12, 13, 16, 17, 20, 21
spines, 7
sprint, 4, 8
sprint in action, 9
stoop, 20
stoop in action, 20
swim, 4, 13
tails, 7, 19
wings, 17, 19, 21

The images in this book are reproduced through the courtesy of: Sumaira35, front cover, p. 6; SunnyS, p. 3; Stuart Westmorland/ Danita Delimont, pp. 4, 10; Welshboy2020, p. 5; Stefonlinton, p. 7 (inset); Frank Wiechens, p. 7 (class: mammal); Rob Schultz, p. 8 (claws); stuporter, pp. 8-9; Danita Delimont, p. 9 (sprint in action!); SeaTops/ Alamy Stock Photo, p. 11 (inset); Doug Perrine/ Alamy Stock Photo, p. 11 (class: fish); Nature Picture Library/ Alamy Stock Photo, pp. 12, 15 (inset), 17; Doug Perrine/ Alamy Stock Photo, p. 13; dizfunkshinal/ Wikipedia, p. 14 (bat background); Phil, p. 14 (free tailed bat); U.S. Fish and Wildlife Service Headquarters/ Wikipedia, p. 15 (class: mammal); Image Source Limited/ Alamy Stock Photo, p. 16; Siepmann/ imageBROKER, p. 17 (moth); imageBROKER.com GmbH & Co. KG/ Alamy Stock Photo, p. 18; Harry Collins, p. 19 (inset); Kamil, p. 19 (class: bird); Ishani, p. 20 (stoop in action!); Dennis Jacobsen, p. 21; kojihirano, p. 22.